# THE MESSIAH

## THE TEXTS BEHIND HANDEL'S MASTERPIECE

## DOUGLAS CONNELLY

8 STUDIES
FOR INDIVIDUALS
OR GROUPS

Life
Builder
Study

# Contents

understanding and appreciation of who Jesus is. You will gain new insight into Jesus' character and power. You will see his whole career plotted out in the ancient writings of Israel.

These passages have had a profound effect on the imagination and worship of Christians for two thousand years. One of the greatest expressions of worship and adoration was written by George Handel. He called his oratorio *Messiah*. We hear it (or parts of it) sung every year during the Christmas season. What many listeners fail to realize is that the entire text of Handel's *Messiah* is drawn from Scripture—and it includes many of the Old Testament passages that shaped Israel's hope for their Redeemer.

So, while the focus of this study guide will be on the biblical passages about the coming Messiah, you will also have the option of exploring sections of Handel's adaptation of some of these passages in *Messiah*. I hope you will play a recording of the significant sections or sing those sections as part of your Bible study.

If you work through this study near the time of Advent or Easter, it will prepare your heart in a fresh way for those celebrations. But any time of the year, these studies will draw you closer to Jesus in adoration and appreciation. Be open to all that God desires to do in you as you take a long look at your Redeemer and Savior and King.

## Suggestions for Individual Study

**1.** As you begin each study, pray that God will speak to you through his Word.

**2.** Read the introduction to the study and respond to the personal reflection question or exercise. This is designed to help you focus on God and on the theme of the study.

**3.** Each study deals with a particular passage so that you can delve into the author's meaning in that context. Read and reread the passage to be studied. The questions are written using the language of the New International Version, so you may wish to use that version of the Bible. The New Revised Standard Version is also recommended.

**4.** This is an inductive Bible study, designed to help you discover for yourself what Scripture is saying. The study includes three types of questions. Observation questions ask about the basic facts: who, what, when, where and how. Interpretation questions delve into the meaning of the passage. Application questions help you discover the implications of the text for growing in Christ. These three keys unlock the treasures of Scripture.

Write your answers to the questions in the spaces provided or in a personal journal. Writing can bring clarity and deeper understanding of yourself and of God's Word.

**5.** It might be good to have a Bible dictionary handy. Use it to look up any unfamiliar words, names or places.

**6.** Use the prayer suggestion to guide you in thanking God for what you have learned and to pray about the applications that have come to mind.

**7.** You may want to go on to the suggestion under "Now or Later," or you may want to use that idea for your next study.

### Suggestions for Members of a Group Study

**1.** Come to the study prepared. Follow the suggestions for individual study mentioned above. You will find that careful preparation will greatly enrich your time spent in group discussion.

**2.** Be willing to participate in the discussion. The leader of your group will not be lecturing. Instead, he or she will be encouraging the members of the group to discuss what they have learned. The leader will be asking the questions that are found in this guide.

**3.** Stick to the topic being discussed. Your answers should be based on the verses which are the focus of the discussion and not

# 1

# His Name Is Wonderful

## Messiah's Character

Isaiah 9:6-7

We are all interested in names. Not long ago the world waited in anticipation to hear a royal baby's official name. We don't number our children; we name them. Names demonstrate our uniqueness and our personhood. One of the greatest compliments we can give another person is to call them by name.

Our names may link us to a grandparent or may be a favorite name chosen by our parents, but they don't have much significance beyond identifying us. That is not true with most biblical names—and especially with the names God gives to himself. God's names and titles reflect his character; they reveal what God is like.

GROUP DISCUSSION. Tell the group something about your name (or a nickname) and why you like or dislike your name.

PERSONAL REFLECTION. What name would God give you if he were to describe your character? What name would you give

**Now or Later**

George Frideric Handel's *Messiah* is a musical phenomenon. Every year this masterful piece is performed hundreds of times by everyone from well-rehearsed choirs with scores of voices to "join in where you can" community sing-alongs.

Handel's work belongs to the musical genre of oratorio. Like operas, oratorios are dramatic stories set entirely to music for soloists, choir or chorus, and orchestra. Unlike opera, oratorios do not include acting, costumes or stage scenery. Oratorios usually tell sacred stories drawn from the Bible or the lives of Christian saints.

*Messiah* is a combination of the music of Handel and the text compiled by Charles Jennings. Jennings drew every word from the Bible (sometimes the King James Version and sometimes from the translation used in the Book of Common Prayer).

The Old Testament writers promised that the coming of the Messiah would bring light into the darkness of a world shrouded in sin and death. In part 1, scene 3, section 2 of *Messiah*, darkness gives way to glorious light. The bass soloist sings a wandering melody, depicting our aimless journey in spiritual darkness. But then light begins to pierce the darkness.

The light is the virgin's child, Emmanuel. The scene reaches its climax in the coming of a Redeemer who will scatter the darkness with his presence and power—"for unto us a child is born."

Listen to both the aria ("The people that walked in darkness") and the chorus ("For unto us a child is born"). If you have access to the musical score, sing along with the soloist and the chorus. This is every Christian's story! We have seen the light in the face of Jesus.

# 2

# The Virgin Will Be with Child

## *Messiah's Birth*

Instead of having children of their own, our son and daughter-in-law decided to welcome foster children into their home. They had already adopted one foster child, Joshua, when God brought a change of direction. At our Thanksgiving dinner one year, Kevin and Julie said that they had an announcement to make to the family—Julie was pregnant with their child. We all shouted and cried and laughed at the joyful news. When we met as a family a month later, the pregnant couple said they had another announcement to make. Their ultrasound images were labeled "Baby 1" and "Baby 2"—twins were on the way! This time the announcement was met with stunned silence and then shouts and laughter. Dakota and Autumn made their grand entrance the following May.

GROUP DISCUSSION. Tell a story about your birth or a joyous birth in your extended family. Why is a birth such a hope-filled event?

PERSONAL REFLECTION. What hopes and dreams did you have

**4.** When the Lord's prophet tells the king to ask for a sign that will confirm God's promise, the king refuses to ask for it. So God himself gives Ahaz a sign: a young woman (virgin) in Judah will conceive a child. Before the child is old enough to know right from wrong, what would happen to the nations plotting against Judah (vv. 14-16)?

---

**5.** If you were Ahaz, would you be comforted by or skeptical of this sign from God? Why?

Isaiah's words had a *historical* fulfillment in Isaiah's own day. Within a few months Judah's enemies had withdrawn from Judah. Within three years the kingdom of Israel was destroyed and within twelve years the nation of Aram was conquered— both by a much greater power, the empire of Assyria. But Isaiah's words had significance far beyond his own lifetime. As the writers of the New Testament looked back at Isaiah's prophecies, the Holy Spirit revealed a whole new level of meaning in Isaiah's words. There was also a *prophetic* fulfillment of these words in the birth of the promised Messiah seven hundred years after Isaiah spoke them. *Read Matthew 1:18-25.*

---

**6.** How would you describe Joseph's feelings toward Mary?

How would you describe Joseph's relationship with the Lord?

# 3

# The Lame Will Walk

## *Messiah's Miracles*

If I could have one gift of God's power, it would be the power to heal. What a thrill it would be to touch a young boy's arm ravaged by cancer and to see that arm made whole! I've prayed for people to be healed and have seen some wonderful demonstrations of God's healing work, but I would like to be able to be the channel through which God would empty hospital wards and cancer clinics by his healing power.

GROUP DISCUSSION. What would you do if you were given the gift of God's healing power for one hour—and what would be the potential dangers of possessing healing ability?

PERSONAL REFLECTION. Where in your life do you need God's healing—in a relationship? In your body? From past failures? Open your heart to the Lord as you begin this study and ask him to begin the healing process.

The prophet Isaiah, more than any other Old Testament

prophet, was given a picture of what the world would look like when God's promised Redeemer would come. One of the prominent marks of God's presence in the Messiah would be the reversal of sin's curse in the lives of those he touched. *Read Isaiah 35:3-6.*

---

**1.** Describe the spiritual and emotional condition of the people Isaiah is addressing (vv. 3-4).

What stress factors in your life right now are causing your hands and knees to tremble or your heart to fear?

---

**2.** What kinds of events will happen to the land and the people God saves (vv. 5-6)?

---

**3.** Which of these miraculous acts seems most difficult and why?

**8.** In what ways might Jesus demonstrate this aspect of his messiahship in your life?

---

**9.** What would you ask him to touch or heal or restore first?

*Ask Jesus to infuse your life with his power and encouragement.*

### Now or Later

Part 1, scene 5 of Handel's *Messiah* tells some of the wonderful things that will happen as a result of the Messiah's birth. Israel will rejoice and find peace in Messiah's eventual reign as king. Isaiah 35:3-6 is spoken just as the Isaiah 7:14 passage—"the virgin will conceive"—was spoken (see study 2). The miracles of Isaiah 35 are followed by the aria, "He shall feed His flock," in which Jesus is portrayed as our comforting shepherd. The aria ends with an invitation, sung by the soprano: "Come unto Him, all ye that labour and are heavy laden, and He will give you rest."

Take the time to listen to the entire scene 5 of part 1. Think about Jesus' care for you and his gracious invitation to rest in him.

Does it help to know that Jesus felt the same way? Explain.

_____

**3.** What does the righteous sufferer in the psalm draw upon for assurance and comfort (vv. 3-5)?

_____

**4.** What past acts of God's faithfulness can you draw upon when you feel like God is far from you?

_____

**5.** Which is worse: feeling abandoned by God or enduring the insults of other people (vv. 6-8)? Why?

_____

**6.** Is this sufferer an evil person living under the consequences of his own rebellion? (Read his testimony in verses 9-11.) Why then has he been rejected?

_____

**7.** From what you know of Jesus' crucifixion, point out details in verses 12-18 that picture the death Jesus would die.

_____

**8.** How does the psalm describe the physical condition of the sufferer (vv. 14-17)?

What might you conclude about the guilt or innocence of an individual in this condition?

---

**9.** What can you learn from verses 19-21 about the attitude of Jesus during his agony on the cross?

How does his example encourage you in your difficult days?

*Express your pain or sorrow or discouragement honestly to the Lord. Follow that with expressions of confident trust in him. You might even pray verses 19-21 to the Lord.*

### Now or Later

The second section of scene 1, part 2 of Handel's *Messiah* takes us to the cross. We hear the abusive shouts of onlookers and the mockery of the crowd. Jesus looked for some to have pity on him but found none. The music and the text are designed to break our hearts. The tenor soloist sings "Behold" four times— "Behold, and see if there be any sorrow like unto His sorrow."

Listen to the last part of scene 1, part 2 in a quiet setting. Let the music sweep over you and let the words break up any hard places in your heart of indifference or rebellion or unresponsiveness to the Lord.

As God began to reveal aspects of the coming Messiah's character and ministry to the Old Testament prophets, one mark of the Messiah became shockingly clear: he would suffer more deeply than any other human being. Most people didn't like that part of the Messiah's ministry. They liked the victorious conqueror side of God's Anointed One and the miracles of healing and power, but not so much the suffering side.

Isaiah saw the Messiah in his glory, but he also got a long, painful look at the Messiah's humiliation. In Isaiah 53 the servant of the Lord (Isaiah 52:13) is despised by his own people and struck down by his own Father. *Read Isaiah 53:1-10.*

---

**1.** If this passage was all we had in the Bible about God's promised Redeemer, what qualities would you look for in someone who claimed to be the Messiah?

Do you find those qualities in Jesus? Explain.

---

**2.** According to verse 2, how would you describe the Messiah's childhood if he grew up next door to you?

---

**3.** How did Isaiah picture the treatment of the Messiah by the people around him (vv. 3, 7-8)?

---

**4.** Those who looked on as the Messiah suffered would consider him stricken down by God in judgment for his own sins (v. 4),

# 6

# The Path of Life

## *Messiah's Resurrection*

**Psalm 16:7-11; Acts 2:22-32**

I've had to do a lot of thinking about the future lately. As I look down the road of life, I see some big changes coming and I've been wrestling with the uncertainties of it all—how to take care of an aging mother, what the next step is in my career, whether we will have the financial resources to help our kids and grandkids. At the same time, I have a peace about the future that only comes from knowing the Lord. He has never failed to care for us in times of plenty and in times of struggle. We have promises that extend throughout life and even far beyond. Jesus will never forsake us, and even death cannot separate us from the love of Christ.

GROUP DISCUSSION. What are some of your concerns as you look at your future? What experiences in the past help to calm your heart about the future?

PERSONAL REFLECTION. When you think of death, do you change the subject? Tremble inside? Have a sense of confidence? Why do you feel the way you do?

David wrote Psalm 16 as he thought about the whole scope of his life. God had blessed him in wonderful ways and surrounded him with godly people. David had faced his share of enemies but God had always seen him through. Even when David thought about his final enemy, death, he knew that God would show him the path of life forever. What David may not have realized as he wrote is that the words of his psalm had far greater significance than just for David. He spoke as a prophet about a greater king yet to come. *Read Psalm 16:7-11.*

---

**1.** As you read back through this short passage again, what was David confident of from the Lord?


---

**2.** What did David do to have such a confident view of life and the future (v. 8)?


---

**3.** Which of David's assertions are you most confident of for your life?



Which are you not so confident about?


---

**4.** What specifically did David believe about his existence and relationship with God beyond death (vv. 10-11)?

in the sacred writings of the Old Testament. The fulfillment of that promise was confirmed by the eyewitness testimony of the apostles. Why do *you* believe that Jesus rose from the dead?

*Pray that the reality of Jesus' resurrection will give you great confidence in God's presence in your personal future—in this life and beyond this life.*

### Now or Later

The moment of Jesus' death is simply announced in *Messiah*, part 2, scene 2—"He was cut off out of the land of the living" (Isaiah 53:8). But death was not the end for Jesus. There is no musical account in *Messiah* of Jesus' burial or the earthquake or the women at the tomb. Instead the resurrection is proclaimed in the words of Psalm 16:10—"But Thou didst not leave His soul in hell." The minor keys of scene 1 give way to major keys in scene 2. Jens Larsen writes: "From the beginning of the aria we are in a new world, above all earthly torment and death, freed from darkness and the oppression of hell" (Jens Peter Larsen, *Handel's Messiah: Origins, Composition, Sources* [New York: W. W. Norton, 1957], p. 150).

As you listen to scene 2, enter into the joy of Jesus' resurrection. Because death was not the end for him, neither will it be for us.

**4.** The imagery of verses 7-10 is of a victorious king returning to Jerusalem in triumph. What aspects of this great king's character does David emphasize?

_____

**5.** How does this entrance of a mighty king contrast with Jesus' first coming to earth?

_____

**6.** In what ways can we acknowledge and celebrate the majesty and authority of Jesus in our lives?

_____

**7.** How can we display Jesus' glory and majesty in our corporate worship?

Do you leave the worship service at your church with the realization that you have been in the presence of the King of glory? Why or why not?

*Express your allegiance and loyalty to Jesus as King. Humble yourself before him with your words and actions.*

### Now or Later

As we've seen in this study, verses 7-10 of Psalm 24 depict the return of a victorious king from battle. The Messiah, the King of glory, returns to the splendor of heaven in victory over sin, Satan and death.

The chorus Handel composed to celebrate Jesus' ascension is unique among the choruses of *Messiah*; it is the work's only antiphonal chorus. The higher voices of the choir announce the King's coming; the lower voices respond with the question, "Who is the King of glory?" Back and forth the voices ring in a stirring anthem of praise.

Listen to (or sing) part 2, scene 3 ("Lift up your heads, O ye gates") with joy-filled enthusiasm. Picture Jesus returning to heaven and reclaiming his place of majesty and authority at God's right hand.

GROUP DISCUSSION. Tell the group about a time when the words or majesty of a song caused you to respond in some outward way—stand, kneel, applaud, weep, raise your hands. Who were you responding to?

PERSONAL REFLECTION. What is your normal posture in worship? In prayer? What might a new posture express to the Lord?

The writers of the Old Testament not only caught a glimpse of a suffering Messiah and a victorious Messiah, they also saw a coming Messiah. God's promised Redeemer would burst out of heaven and reclaim all that Adam had lost. The Messiah would take back his world, rescue his people and destroy his enemies. The prophet Daniel watched a series of evil wild beasts stalk the earth, ravishing God's people and crushing all who stood against them. Suddenly Daniel's eyes were drawn to heaven and a very different scene unfolded there. God was about to reclaim what was rightly his. *Read Daniel 7:9-14.*

---

**1.** Daniel sees a powerful figure seated on heaven's throne, "the Ancient of Days." What does each element of Daniel's description convey to you about the character and ability of this heavenly being?

Clothing:

Hair:

Throne:

River:

Attendants:

Which name gives you the most confidence as you face tomorrow? Explain.

*Compose a song or shout of praise to Jesus for his goodness, grace and power in your life. Sing or read it to the group—and to the Lord as an act of worship.*

### Now or Later

In Handel's *Messiah* the famous "Hallelujah Chorus" immediately follows the account of Christ's victory over his enemies. Some have called this section a "coronation anthem" in which Jesus is revealed as the King over all kings. In three and a half minutes Handel packs all the jubilation and pomp necessary for such an occasion. The passage reaches a stirring climax with the phrases "King of Kings" and "He shall reign" echoing over and over. Then comes a flurry of eight "forevers" and "hallelujahs," a grand pause, and the final powerful "Hal-le-lu-jah!"

If your group can sing (or wants to try), pass out the score of the "Hallelujah Chorus" and let everyone sing along with the recorded version (standing, of course). You might also put together a small orchestra and choir, and sing the piece as part of your worship service at your church. It's traditionally sung at Christmas or Easter but can be sung any time as an expression of praise and adoration to Jesus.

# Leader's Notes

Leading a Bible discussion can be an enjoyable and rewarding experience. But it can also be *scary*—especially if you've never done it before. If this is your feeling, you're in good company. When God asked Moses to lead the Israelites out of Egypt, he replied, "O Lord, please send someone else to do it!" (Ex 4:13). It was the same with Solomon, Jeremiah and Timothy, but God helped these people in spite of their weaknesses, and he will help you as well.

You don't need to be an expert on the Bible or a trained teacher to lead a Bible discussion. The idea behind these inductive studies is that the leader guides group members to discover for themselves what the Bible has to say. This method of learning will allow group members to remember much more of what is said than a lecture would.

These studies are designed to be led easily. As a matter of fact, the flow of questions through the passage from observation to interpretation to application is so natural that you may feel that the studies lead themselves. This study guide is also flexible. You can use it with a variety of groups—student, professional, neighborhood or church groups. Each study takes forty-five to sixty minutes in a group setting.

There are some important facts to know about group dynamics and encouraging discussion. The suggestions listed below should enable you to effectively and enjoyably fulfill your role as leader.

when people have difficulty understanding or answering a question. Third, the leader's notes can alert you to potential problems you may encounter during the study.

**10.** If you wish to remind yourself of anything mentioned in the leader's notes, make a note to yourself below that question in the study.

## Leading the Study

**1.** Begin the study on time. Open with prayer, asking God to help the group to understand and apply the passage.

**2.** Be sure that everyone in your group has a study guide. Encourage the group to prepare beforehand for each discussion by reading the introduction to the guide and by working through the questions in the study.

**3.** At the beginning of your first time together, explain that these studies are meant to be discussions, not lectures. Encourage the members of the group to participate. However, do not put pressure on those who may be hesitant to speak during the first few sessions. You may want to suggest the following guidelines to your group.

☐ Stick to the topic being discussed.

☐ Your responses should be based on the verses which are the focus of the discussion and not on outside authorities such as commentaries or speakers.

☐ These studies focus on a particular passage of Scripture. Only rarely should you refer to other portions of the Bible. This allows for everyone to participate in in-depth study on equal ground.

☐ Anything said in the group is considered confidential and will not be discussed outside the group unless specific permission is given to do so.

☐ We will listen attentively to each other and provide time for each person present to talk.

☐ We will pray for each other.

**4.** Have a group member read the introduction at the beginning of the discussion.

group. Ask for God's help in following through on the commitments you've made.

**18.** End on time.

Many more suggestions and helps are found in *How to Lead a LifeBuilder Study.*

## Components of Small Groups

A healthy small group should do more than study the Bible. There are four components to consider as you structure your time together.

*Nurture.* Small groups help us to grow in our knowledge and love of God. Bible study is the key to making this happen and is the foundation of your small group.

*Community.* Small groups are a great place to develop deep friendships with other Christians. Allow time for informal interaction before and after each study. Plan activities and games that will help you get to know each other. Spend time having fun together going on a picnic or cooking dinner together.

*Worship and prayer.* Your study will be enhanced by spending time praising God together in prayer or song. Pray for each other's needs and keep track of how God is answering prayer in your group. Ask God to help you to apply what you are learning in your study.

*Outreach.* Reaching out to others can be a practical way of applying what you are learning, and it will keep your group from becoming self-focused. Host a series of evangelistic discussions for your friends or neighbors. Clean up the yard of an elderly friend. Serve at a soup kitchen together, or spend a day working in the community.

Many more suggestions and helps in each of these areas are found in the *Small Group Starter Kit.* You will also find information on building a small group. Reading through the starter kit will be worth your time.

**Study 1. His Name Is Wonderful. Isaiah 9:6-7.**

*Purpose:* To introduce Jesus as the Messiah and to explore his incredible character.

**Question 1.** The person Isaiah talks about is called a "child" and a "son." He is a human child who is "born." This child will also reign on David's throne over an earthly kingdom. But Isaiah uses other phrases to describe this person that make him more than human. He will reign but his kingdom will have "no end," and he will rule "forever." How can a mere human child also be called "Mighty God"?

**Questions 2-3.** The first title given to this promised one is "Wonderful Counselor." The first person we call or turn to in a crisis is the person we trust the most. Where the Lord fits on that list of those we go to in a time of need tells us how much we have learned to rely on Jesus as our Counselor and Guide. Jesus usually guides us through his Word, but he may also direct us by the Spirit, by circumstances or by insights that come from faith.

**Question 5.** When we are linked by faith to Jesus, we enjoy eternal blessings immediately. The believer has eternal life—a whole new kind of life lived in a new realm. We are indwelt by God's eternal Spirit and learn what it means to be directed by him. The Christian is "in Christ" and Christ is "in us," so we have access to a person who is the source of wisdom and right decisions.

**Question 7.** This is the first of several questions in this study guide in which the participant is asked to reflect on his or her personal belief or relationship with the Lord and to reveal possible areas of struggle or doubt. You, the leader, need to give each person the freedom and safety to answer without fear of judgment or condemnation from you or any other group member. When difficult issues are expressed, approach them with compassion and understanding. The goal is to help each person work through these areas of struggle with the Lord's help.

**Question 8.** Isaiah saw the glory of the Messiah's kingdom more

of the prophecy (v. 8), the nation that now threatened Judah would be just a memory. Ahaz's responsibility was to believe what God had said and to remain faithful to the Lord. If Ahaz sought help from any other source, his kingdom would fall.

**Question 4.** Isaiah uses the Hebrew word *'almah* to refer to a young and probably unmarried woman at the time. By the time this woman conceives a child and gives birth, and the child can discern between what is harmful to him and what is not harmful, about three years would elapse. By then the two invading kings would be gone from Judean soil. In Matthew's translation of Isaiah 7:14 in Matthew 1:23, he uses the Greek word *parthenos* which specifically means a virgin woman.

Stan Guthrie adds, "Jews in Joseph's (Mary's promised husband) time probably saw Isaiah 7:14 as both fulfilled in the prophet's life and also as a larger messianic prediction. . . . Therefore, Jews such as Joseph viewed this prediction as having a larger, miraculous fulfillment—Immanuel, *God*, would be with them" (Stan Guthrie, *A Concise Guide to Bible Prophecy* [Grand Rapids: Baker, 2013], p. 91).

**Question 5.** Both the sign and the fulfillment required Ahaz to wait. All he had to rely on was the word of the Lord through Isaiah the prophet. God used this experience as a test for Ahaz and the people of Judah—would they trust God even if it took a while, or would they seek immediate help from another direction and forfeit God's blessing? We face the same struggle when we trust God to work in a problem situation or relationship rather than plunging in on our own.

**Question 6.** Joseph loved Mary and didn't want to see her publicly humiliated. At the same time, Joseph was a righteous man. He knew that he was not the father of Mary's child, and so he could only come to one conclusion—that Mary had been unfaithful to him. Joseph's relationship to the Lord is revealed in his willingness to believe the angel's message and his immediate obedience to what the angel told him to do.

**Questions 8-9**. Jesus may choose to work in our lives in miraculous power or he may choose not to. The point is that Jesus' new life and power are available to us. Even if we feel imprisoned by current circumstances, we are called to trust him fully and to look with eager anticipation for his intervention in our lives.

### Study 4. Why Have You Forsaken Me? Psalm 22:1-21.

*Purpose:* To see Jesus as our model for facing suffering with confident trust in God.

**Introduction.** Psalm 22 is the first passional psalm—a song that reflects extreme suffering. Psalms 35, 41, 55, 69, and 109 are also passional psalms. Psalm 22 is quoted more often in the New Testament than any other psalm, but the author is never identified in the New Testament quotations. David's authorship is confirmed by the heading of the psalm.

Walter Kaiser summarizes the view of most evangelical interpreters of Psalm 22: "David did experience unusual suffering, but under a revelation from God he witnesses the suffering of one of his offspring, presumably the last in that promised line, that far transcends anything that came his way" (Walter Kaiser, *The Messiah in the Old Testament* [Grand Rapids: Zondervan, 1995], p. 113).

**Question 1.** The sufferer feels abandoned by God, but that feeling does not mesh with what the writer knows about the character and past actions of the Lord. The writer knows God has been faithful to respond to his people and to rescue them from trouble (vv. 4-5), but at the same time he feels like God is ignoring him now (v. 2). God is his strength (v. 19), but the writer is close to death (v. 15).

**Question 2.** David's question in verse 1 (and Jesus' echo of the same question as he hung on the cross) is not a question of surprise or doubt. It's an exclamation, a rhetorical question. He is not seeking an answer as much as he is standing in shocked awe that such an event would ever happen. What circumstance in God's plan would bring him to abandon someone who had been faithful to him?

**Questions 3-4.** As the sufferer thinks back over the biblical story, he can recall example after example in which God intervened to rescue those who were in danger or in pain. These spiritual ancestors cried out to the Lord and the Lord responded quickly and powerfully. God's faithful acts in the past brought encouragement as the sufferer patiently waited for God's deliverance.

**Question 6.** There had to be some other explanation for the righteous person's suffering. It simply could not be secret sin or moral corruption. If he was not standing under God's judgment for his own sin, there had to be another purpose for the suffering he was enduring. In Jesus' case, he was suffering God's judgment in the place of others. Those looking on were drawing an easy conclusion about the sufferer, but it was the wrong conclusion.

**Question 7.** Even those with only a basic knowledge of Jesus' crucifixion should be able to point out a few details: crowds of soldiers and enemies surrounded the cross (vv. 12-13; see Mt 27:36-44; Lk 23:35-39); crucifixion was a torturous death (v. 14); Jesus suffered intense thirst (v. 15; see Jn 19:28); Jesus' hands and feet were pierced (v. 16; see Jn 20:27); Jesus hung virtually naked on the cross (v. 17); soldiers gambled for Jesus' clothes (v. 18; see Mt 27:35; Jn 19:23-24).

**Question 8.** The conclusion most onlookers came to as they witnessed Jesus' crucifixion was that he was dying under the curse and penalty of God for his blasphemy. Even today some people (including some Christians) look at a person in physical decline or illness and wonder what that person has done to deserve such treatment from God. Other Christians conclude (correctly, I think) that a suffering person is sharing in experiences common to all of us and that God may use physical illness to strengthen our faith and trust in him.

**Question 9.** In spite of the crushing pain of the cross, Jesus maintained his trust and confidence in his Father. He knew that when the sin-bearing was finished, the Father would come quickly to

the leaders of Israel looked on his death as the evidence of God's curse on Jesus. When Jesus had the opportunity speak in his own defense, he usually stood in silence. In the minds of most people then and now, this suffering Messiah can hardly be the one who will deliver us from the bondage of sin and death.

**Question 4.** "The sufferings of the Servant were not his own fault, as 'we' thought, but were in fact the result of 'our' sins, and resulted in 'our' healing" (Oswalt, p. 384). Jesus was carrying "the iniquity of us all" in his body on the cross.

**Question 5.** The imagery of sacrifice and the substitution of the righteous for the guilty pervades Isaiah's thoughts. Jesus did not simply die for a noble cause or as the result of misplaced justice. Jesus died in our place, in our stead, and because of his sacrifice the penalty of our sin has been fully paid forever. He died for sinners, not as a martyr for a cause.

**Question 6.** The writers of the New Testament interpreted the historical event of Jesus' execution through the lens of Old Testament sacrifice and through the insight given by the Holy Spirit. Jesus' death was the ultimate sacrifice for sin. He was made sin for us and was given the treatment we deserved before God. His suffering, pain and death bring spiritual healing to us who deserve God's wrath, not his grace.

**Question 7.** Jesus' death for sinners was the supreme expression of God's love for lost human beings. We deserved separation from God, but God himself made a way for the penalty of sin to be paid and, at the same time, to rescue believing sinners.

**Question 8.** The Servant persisted in doing the will of his Father even when it brought rejection, dismissal and death. We as followers of Jesus are called to follow him with the same willingness to sacrifice our lives for others. We need to remember too that just as Jesus was exalted because of his faithful endurance in suffering (Phil 2:8-9), we will also receive God's reward for patient endurance (Jas 1:12).

two elements. The promised Messiah would not experience the decay of his body like David did, but would be raised from the dead before decay set in. We no longer hear the testimony of the eyewitnesses to the resurrection as the early Christians did, but we can read their testimony in written form preserved for us in the Bible. We also have the inner witness of the Holy Spirit who confirms the truth of the gospel to us, but that inner witness rests on the objective testimony of God's Word.

### Study 7. Lift Up Your Heads. Psalm 24.

*Purpose:* To reaffirm our submission to Jesus as our mighty Lord and King.

**Question 1.** God's creation of the world, his ultimate ownership of all that is in it and his sovereign authority over all who live in it give us the context for appreciating God's majesty. The Lord is not some minor deity or a god with limitations. The Lord reigns over all. No being is greater or higher than he is.

**Questions 2-3.** David wrote in the context of the ark of the covenant, the place of God's visible presence with his people. Therefore, to come into God's immediate presence required worshipers to literally ascend to the city of Jerusalem and to present themselves in the place designated by God for worship. In this age, however, we can come confidently into God's presence anywhere. This passage is not just about coming to church. It is about making conscious preparation whenever or wherever we approach God in worship. Our hearts and lives are examined and our sins are confessed and our spirits are open to offer adoration to the Lord and to receive the blessings he desires to give. Our trust is in the Lord alone.

**Question 4.** Having gathered in the place of worship, the worshipers anticipate the arrival of the Lord himself. The command to "lift up your head" is symbolic of looking up in anticipation and hope. The gates of the city "look up" in preparation for the arrival of the great king. David emphasizes the power and greatness of the one who will arrive. We know this great king as Jesus Christ, who has been exalted to the highest place and given a name that is above every other name (Phil 2:9).

**Question 5.** Jesus' first coming to earth was quiet and humble, hardly the entrance of a great king. He was largely ignored and dismissed by his own people. He made his entrance into Jerusalem on a donkey, surrounded by peasant followers. Jesus' second coming to earth, on the other hand, will be far different. He will arrive as the King over all kings (Rev 19:11-16).

**Question 6.** Jesus already reigns in heaven and over his church as God's King. He also reigns as Lord in the hearts and lives of believers. We may not always live as if Jesus is Lord, but he is. As we submit ourselves to his authority and live as his loyal subjects, we display Jesus' glory to the people around us.

**Question 7.** We regularly acknowledge Jesus' friendship and love and grace in our worship. I wonder sometimes if we see or sing or acknowledge much of his majesty or authority over us as Lord and King. The purpose of the final question is not to criticize a particular style of worship but to examine our own attitudes and actions in worship. Do we sense that we stand together with other believers in the presence of our conquering King? Do we submit ourselves fully to him and to his Word in our worship? Are we casually comfortable or waiting in hopeful anticipation for the arrival of the King of glory?

### Study 8. The Clouds of Heaven. Daniel 7:9-14; Revelation 19:1-16.

*Purpose:* To stir our hearts to joyful anticipation of Jesus' return.

**Question 1.** You may want to take a *Pictionary* approach to this question. As you talk about each element in the vision, have a different group member add it to the composite picture and then discuss what that element communicates to you about the character and power of the heavenly being. The person seen by Daniel can only be God, but Daniel only sees a visual representation of God. This isn't what God looks like since God the Father has no body

evil and oppression, we also have the confidence that God will one day bring his perfect justice to bear on those who are wicked and corrupt. They may seem to escape justice now, but they won't escape forever.

**Question 5.** The "shouts" in this chapter all originate in heaven. These are the words of angels and redeemed believers in heaven as they see God's great plan of redemption come to its climax in the return of Jesus to earth in power and glory. God is pictured as the sovereign King bringing judgment on the wicked and deliverance to the righteous. All his servants in heaven rejoice because the time of the wedding of the Lamb to his bride has finally come. You may want to read this passage as the narrator with the group members reading (or shouting!) the five expressions of praise.

**Question 6.** Group members may see themselves in more than one place in the passage. Any who see themselves as being struck down under God's wrath should be encouraged to seek or to rest in God's grace and forgiveness through faith in Jesus.

**Question 7.** No matter what trials or opposition or persecution we face today as Christians, we know how the story ends. Jesus will overcome—and we are in his hands.

**Question 8.** Several descriptive titles are given to Jesus in these verses—"Faithful and True," the "Word of God," "King of kings and Lord of lords." All the titles are designed to remind us of his future victory and ultimate triumph over every enemy. If you have time, encourage the group members to use the title that gives them the most confidence to address Jesus in prayer or in an expression of praise.

---

*Douglas Connelly (MDiv and MTh, Grace Theological Seminary) is the senior pastor at Davison Missionary Church, near Flint, Michigan. He is also the author of* Angels Around Us *(InterVarsity Press) and* The Bible for Blockheads *(Zondervan), as well as seventeen LifeBuilder Bible Studies.*